Memoirs of a Foster Child

by Louise DeStefano

DORRANCE PUBLISHING CO
EST. 1920
PITTSBURGH, PENNSYLVANIA 15238

Dorrance Publishing Co
585 Alpha Drive
Pittsburgh, PA 15238
Visit our website at *www.dorrancebookstore.com*

ISBN: 979-8-8860-4082-1
eISBN: 979-8-8860-4981-7

Memoirs of a Foster Child

Table of Contents

"The Tiny House"

In 1950 on Sunrise Highway, one of many highways on Long Island, you could see so many lots full of trees and shrubs all over the place. Today, it is mostly shopping centers, industrial buildings, and homes. Set back along this highway surrounded by a lot of land, at least so it seemed with me being only four at the time, was a tiny three-room house called home. I lived there with my twin sister and my older brother John, along with my mom. Much of what I remember of this tiny house is that it had only one bedroom, a tiny room attached, and a living room and dining room combined.

The bedroom had only a full-size bed in which we all slept, including my mom. The tiny room was the size of a bathroom, without any toilet or plumbing; it only had a full-length mirror in it where my mom spent a lot of time in front of. In the living room, we had a pot belly stove to heat the entire tiny house, and I guess it did because I do not remember being cold. My brother had to find firewood and sometimes we had coal for it. We also had an icebox to keep our food cold, and I remember the big block of ice always being delivered. We did not know what it was like to have hot water, because the water we did have came from a hand pump in the sink that had to be primed each time it was used.

We had no indoor bathroom so we used an outhouse in the back of the house. I hated it because it smelled so bad and had bugs and flies all over. Additionally, it was filled to the top, so I would find a spot in the woods, even though I was so scared of someone seeing me.

Some memories are vague of my short time in this tiny house, which was home at the time. I remember sitting with my twin and my mom hitting us to stay awake, and I never knew why. Another time, we were forced to eat mashed potatoes that tasted like the entire container of salt was poured into them, and I was really thirsty after that. Water was not something easily available to us. I remember one time I was so thirsty, I went into my mom's tiny mirror room and saw a glass filled with water on the window sill. I picked it up and drank it down; what a mistake! It tasted awful. It turns out it was the water my mom dipped her hair comb in. I never did that again. I was only four at the time, though, what did I know? I was still thirsty all the time, so I discovered an old rusty chest in the back of the tiny house filled with water from the rain. I bent down and sipped as much water as I could without caring that it had rust particles; it was so good. At times, I would go outside for a drink, even when it was pitch black out. I was more thirsty than scared.

One day while I was in my mom's mirror room dressing, my mom stood there watching me, with an evil look on her face and said to me that my body was different than other girls. What a thing to say to a four-year-old, at such an impressionable age. This stayed with me for a long time, until I was much older and was told I was not different, I was normal like other girls.

On the large property where we lived in the tiny house was a large broken-down vacant house my sister, brother, and I played in and huddled up together to stay warm. We had to play outside when it was cold for most of the day.

At four years old, I would sit on my front steps of the tiny house and gaze across sunrise highway to the street that was parallel to it. As I watched mothers push their baby carriages, which today are antiques, and they had hoods and a large area for the babies to sleep. I would look at the back of these carriages coming toward me and get this wonderful feeling. I would get that same feeling when I saw a gray limo driving away from me.

Not long ago, actually some years ago, I bought a carriage just like the one the mothers pushed when I was four, because of the feelings and memory that I had. I really do not know what those feelings meant, I can only presume the carriage was a symbol of me having a lot of babies someday and I did. The symbol of the limo might have meant that someday I would be rich, and I am rich with the love of the family I now have. As of today, I still experience the same feeling when I see that carriage and the gray limo.

One fond memory of living in the tiny house was when my sister and I at three years old were each given a beautiful pink and yellow lace dress. When we put them on, we looked like two living dolls that my mom easily got rid of.

"My Dad"

Naturally I only talked about my mom, because I never met my dad. I found out later from my Uncle Jay, my mom's brother, about my dad. Uncle Jay said my dad usually went out for a few beers with friends on Friday nights. After a while, he would go out on Friday and not come home until Monday or Tuesday, and one day he did not come home at all. The Welfare Department tried to find him but nothing ever came of it. I found out later on in my life that he did go to court to try and see us but my mom never told us.

I remember a man sitting on a chair in our living room, really, I am only remembering his knees. I thought it was my dad, but it was not. It was a man of the few men my mom entertained. He stood out in my mind because he told me beans are good for your heart so the more you eat the more you will ———— the better you will feel so eat beans at every meal, not something appropriate to say to four-year olds, and my mom never intervened.

Not having a dad made me very easy to be told what to do by my boyfriends. I loved when they got jealous, because I thought it showed they cared. I had no independence or any backbone. Doing everything that my boyfriends told me was like having a dad telling me what to do and not to do, I loved it, and I never knew any different. I always envied other families that consisted of a mom and dad.

At night as I tried to sleep I would just lay there and day dream of stars on television, like Zorro and Doctor Kildare, who I had a mad crush on, being my dad. I would imagine them scolding me and then I would be punished and sent straight to bed. I loved imagining this, and I would do this every night before I would fall asleep.

I always wondered and still do wonder why we were the unlucky ones not to have a mom or dad to love us and want us like others do. It is something you never forget. A child is a precious gift from God and some people take that gift from God for granted. So many women cannot have children and want them with all their hearts. These are the ones that truly deserve that gift and receive it through adoption or other means, and they do have the love to give. We were not a gift for our mom- we were a burden.

"No Hugs or Kisses"

There were never any hugs or kisses around our house. We did not know what they were. This stemmed from my grandmother; she was a stern German woman who raised her children like it was a job, at least that's what Uncle Jay said.

My sister and I turned five, so it was time for school. My mom at this time was in the kitchen making banana sandwiches for our lunch, along with white powdered donuts for school. "What a good lunch," I thought. We were off to school with our brother to guide us across the big highway and no hug or kiss goodbye from our mom. My brother always watched out for us; he was only seven and had to be the man of the house.

School was good, and we looked okay besides the fact that we were so skinny and kept scratching our heads. It turns out we had head lice and had cakey stuff on the lower part of our scalps so we had to leave school. When we got home, my mom poured kerosene all over our heads to combat the issue, but it did not work. It only smelled horrific.

I only remember one holiday in the tiny house a big truck came and delivered all sorts of toys and clothes for us and Christmas presents. We were so excited. We never had a Christmas tree in the tiny house or any presents, we only had that when we visited our grandmother's house.

"The Lady Visitor"

Not long after the surprise truck delivery, a lady visitor came to our house, and she was from child welfare. The neighbors must have complained that we ran around outside without clothes, looked undernourished, and had bugs in our hair; all of this was true. She talked to our mom for a while and said she would be back to take us for a ride. The day came for the ride to visit a nice family, and we were very excited. We did not know what it was all about, but we loved the idea of going for this ride. The lady of the nice family lived in Copiague on Long Island.

As we pulled up to the house, it looked beautiful and in a real upscale neighborhood. It had four bedrooms and an inside bathroom. We all sat at their kitchen table, along with the lady visitor, who was called a social worker. The lady of the house told us we could call her Aunt Dot, so we did. She offered us cookies and milk and said there was more where that came from so just to ask. It was a nice visit; we stayed a while and then the social worker brought us home to our tiny house.

"No One Wanted Us"

Obviously, we were taken away because our mom could not take care of us. But why wouldn't anyone else in our family take us two beautiful twin girls with big gorgeous eyes? Why wouldn't my godparents step in? Even today, I do not know why. When you appoint godparents to your child or children it stands for something, if the parents of the children cannot take care of them, you have committed to that duty as godparents. Why did our godparents take on this responsibility and not fulfill it?

Oh, and my grandmother who I idolized my entire life did not take us. One time my Uncle Jay, who lived with my grandmother at the time, was asked, "Do you remember when the twin's mom gave them up?" Uncle Jay said, "Yes, that is something that has stayed in my mind forever. Welfare came to my home, and at that time I was the only one left at home in this big house. I was about fourteen or sixteen years of age. Welfare asked my mom if she would take the twins in, but she said she did not have the room. When I questioned her about it later, she was cold and danced around with the answer as she always did, and she finally told me that the welfare would not allow two girls and a boy to live in the same house together. I later realized that was a lie and soon after, the big house burnt down. I guess God works in mysterious ways."

Uncle Jay said he never brought any girls home because his mom, my grandmother, never liked anyone. Uncle Jay was somebody you did not forget; he always took my sister and I for ice cream. He was so young and was not able to take care of us, but he never forgot how we were bounced around and there was not a thing he could do about it, being so young.

As we got older and on with our lives, we still never wanted to be estranged from our real family. No one bothered with my sister and me. We were never invited to family functions, like weddings and so on. The only one who acknowledged us was my older brother and younger brother. They invited us to a few family reunions. I would feel so strange around these people; but the fact was, I belonged there. They were my real family, even though I felt out of place.

At one of these reunions, my mom was there and one of my children had called her grandma, not that she earned it, and she said, "Do not call me that. I am not your grandma." She did not deserve to be called grandma or mom; she was neither.

"The Move"

The social worker explained to us that we would be leaving our mom and brother to live with Aunt Dot. She would take care of us for a little while, and it was only a temporary move. My mom said it will not be for long, and we believed her.

The time came for the move, and my mom was not even sad upon our leaving. We should have expected as much, but we were too little to realize it. We were finally moving to our temporary home at Aunt Dot's and there was no grand greeting. The only plus in our move is that welfare never separated my sister and me. We were always together. Here are some memories that stand out for me of which I will never forget.

When we had breakfast at Aunt Dot's, we sat by this little shelf in the kitchen that barely had enough room for one child and there was not even a table. We were served a half of a piece of toast, and Aunt Dot said if you would like more just ask. We did ask and she said we had enough, much different from our short visit with the social worker.

Soon it was Thanksgiving time to have a feast of food and desserts, but not for us. We sat in the kitchen table eating leftover spaghetti, while the rest of the family had a Thanksgiving feast in their dining room.

Aunt Dot had a son and daughter of her own. I do not remember them too much for we were not included in family functions. The only time we were was when they could not leave us alone in the house, so they brought us along. One of their relatives, an older cousin about maybe nineteen or twenty, used to touch me in places I learned later were supposed to be private.

I remember going to the beach, and he was there he picked me up and straddled me around his waist and it happened again. Aunt Dot's yard had a swing set and while I was swinging on the swing with my sister, the cousin was visiting at Aunt Dot's and came in the back yard and asked me to come in a vacant car sitting in their driveway I thought nothing of it. I was only five or six at the time. He proceeded to touch me again. I did not know what was right or wrong being so young.

As time went on, I thought I did something terrible but I was a victim of this bad man. God only knows how many other children he violated. In my opinion, the family had to know and they covered it up. He had to have done it to some child that was older and wise enough to tell his parents. My sister never mentioned that she was a victim of that man. This time, if the social worker came to move us, it would be the right thing to do under the circumstances.

It is simply outrageous how some families think they can get away with any kind of abuse with foster children because they have in their minds that no one cares and they're not family anyway.

"Holiday at Aunt Dot's"

During our stay at Aunt Dot's, my mom and grandma came once a month to take us out for the day. Our mom always said during our visits that when she gets married again she would take us back. At Christmas, our grandma gave us each a baby doll and we loved them. It turns out, the next morning they disappeared because Aunt Dot gave them to her daughter.

Speaking of my grandma again, the one who did not want us, before I was aware of this I always wanted to be like her someday. To me, she was the best grandma in the whole world. Our mom would pick us up for our monthly visit and go to grandma's, and we would have a great dinner and even a real cup of coffee with a saucer. She made fresh apple pie with the apples from her tree and also made homemade sherbet. One Christmas was very different. When I walked into Grandma's house, there was no smell of Grandpa's cigar, I found out later that he had passed away right after my mom gave us up. Grandpa had no knowledge that my mom, his daughter, had given us to child welfare. He would have been very upset. Grandpa had a greenhouse in the back-yard. He and Uncle Jay took care of it. There were all sorts of veggies and flowers, and I remember going in there and breathing a wonderful smell that would hit me the minute I entered. After Grandpa's passing,

Uncle Jay was just too young to take on the responsibility of maintaining the greenhouse. The greenhouse smell and the smell of a cigar burning left me with wonderful memories of my Grandpa.

At Christmas time, we opened presents and had lots of food and deserts. Grandma also had the most beautiful Christmas tree. It was lit with candles that were filled with water and old vintage ornaments. A small city with benches and people surrounded the awesome tree with a train that ran around it. I would lie underneath the tree and put tinsel on the tracks just to see them spark. To this day, I still try and replicate Grandma's tree.

I remember so clearly the memory of Grandpa sitting in his chair where the Christmas tree was, smoking his cigar and not a gray hair on his head. At Easter time at Grandma's, she made Easter baskets out of tins and Easter eggs that were always dark in color, which made them really stand out. These are all such fond memories that carried me through my growing up years, until one day when I got older to find out the truth about grandma from her own son, Uncle Jay. Also, with these memories, there were still no hugs or kisses or saying "I love you."

There is a phrase that grandmas are the glue that holds the family together, but not in this case. My grand-godson gave me a pillow with that same phrase because I am the glue, unlike my own so-called grandmother. My grandson is also my godson; it is something you do not see every day, but my daughter thinks that much of me and gave me that honor.

"Back to Aunt Dots"

The time always came when we had to leave our real family and go back to the strange Aunt Dot. Since we did not have enough to eat at Aunt Dot's, my sister and I would rummage through the neighbor's garbage, and one day I hit the jackpot and found a blueberry pie that was half-eaten. Our friend brought us tiny loaves of bread, and we would gobble them down outside on her steps in the cold almost every day.

Across the street from Aunt Dot's was an empty lot. It was full of tall grass, a child's playground, and we made make-believe offices and houses. One day, my sister and I started digging in the dirt and we made a large hole. We were having fun. All of a sudden, some guy came over to us and said, Watch when you see a red dot in the dirt, it will turn into a monster and get you!" We were so frightened we had nightmares for a long time and never went back to the tall grass again.

"Lady Visitor, Again (Social Worker)"

The time came when the social worker came to move us again. We were around six or seven and it was to be for our own good. Neighbors saw us always looking through the garbage and asking our friends for food, and then there were the incidents that I experienced with the older cousin, which nobody even knew about, or would even care.

Where did we go next? Good question, and there was no prior visit this time. We moved to a ranch house with pink shutters and a big yard in Wyandanch and it was on a dead end. The new people were called the Eddels, and we were allowed to call them Aunt and Uncle. The uncle was very easy-going, but the aunt was very strict. My sister and I slept in a full-size bed, and their son slept in a twin bed across from us in the same room. Their grandpa also lived there; he had his own room and stayed to himself, and he was kind of grouchy. He watched baseball all the time; I would hear it each time I past his room. Even to this day, every time I hear a baseball game, it brings back memories of him. The Eddels had cookouts with their next-door neighbors, and they put a lot of tables together for all the food. We had a really good time playing with the kids and eating until we were stuffed.

When it was time for school, we walked to the end of our block to the bus stop. While waiting for the bus, the kids would always bully my sister and me. In school, the same thing happened. During gym, one of the girls flushed our slips down the toilet. We never looked forward to going to school because of all the bullying.

The Eddels had a garage built, and I played in there all the time. I loved the smell of the new construction. Their dead end had a swamp behind it, which my sister and I always ventured in and played all day. We got a little wet, but we survived. I was taught to ride a two-wheeler while living here. I do not recall by whom, but what a wonderful feeling when that person let go of the end of the bike and I went on my merry way.

We had a few friends, and one friend was a native of Germany and much older than us played games with us. One day, she told us a true story about the birds and the bees and told us in a very descriptive manner, and it was ugly to hear. We were so young and did not understand. It stayed in our minds for a long time until we learned the correct story sometime later.

While living with the Eddels my mom came once a month to take us for the day, again telling us this is only temporary until she gets married again. We always wanted to go home and live with our mom. Our one-day visit would always take us to Woolworth's fountain, where we would have ice cream or a malted, and by the time we went back to the Eddels we were stuffed with goodies.

The next visit with our mom, she told us we had a new brother. We were confused because she never married again. How could this be? She went on later and had another, but we were just too young to realize how this happened. My older brother was there for it all. She had given birth twice in the tiny house with only my brother there. He was still too young to experience this, but I am sure it stayed on his mind for a long time.

"That Social Worker Again"

Here comes the social worker. I suppose it was time for us to move again. Why else would she come and visit? She never came any other time to see how we were doing in our temporary living arrangement, and yes, we had to move. The reason was that we were sleeping in the same room with their son, and that is not allowed by child welfare.

The social worker said our new home would be with the Harrisons. They lived in West Babylon and had three ducks and a goose. The ducks were called Jack, Jill, and the Pail. With no prior visit, we were ready to leave the Eddels. Mrs. Eddel seemed sad we were leaving, but there was nothing she could do at this point.

"Life With the Harrisons"

My sister and I were eleven years old on our move to the Harrisons, although we looked like we were much younger due to all the prior neglect. The Harrisons tried to fatten us up with really good meals, and we were not undernourished anymore and no more rummaging through the garbage. Oma was their grandmother. Oma stands for grandmother in German. Oma never gave anyone a hard time. She cooked meals and made farina with eggs for our breakfast. It was really good.

Oma had the bedroom alongside of ours upstairs and would hang out and watch television every evening. She would ask me to sneak her a beer because Mr. Harrison did not like her drinking, so I did, and it made her very happy. She was up there in age, and it was not like she was going to be an alcoholic. It just helped her relax and enjoy the night as she laid back on her recliner.

We had friends next door to where we lived at the Harrisons, and one day, I decided to tell the daughter about the birds and the bees as I was taught so wrongly from the German girl back at the Eddels. Well, her mother went to Mrs. Harrison and asked "What kind of riff raff are you raising?" At this time, Mrs. Harrison sat down with my sister and me and explained the correct story of the birds and the bees and read a book to us explaining how a girl becomes a lady.

One day, we were playing outside and our other friend kept on teasing us. I said, "Stop or I will tell my mom," meaning Mrs. Harrison. Mrs. Harrison overheard the conversation and asked us if we would like to call her mom and Mr. Harrison dad, so we agreed. At first, it felt so weird, but after a while, we were okay with it. When I saw my real mom, it felt really strange calling her mom again.

Although I did call Mrs. Harrison mom, she never said she loved us, and still we got no hugs, but she did give us a kiss each night before bed. When you tell a true story, you change the characters names, of which I did. One of the foster families I named the Harrison's as written. One night, I was watching television and a commercial came on about adopting a foster child. The camera first focused on the adopted mom and the foster child, then the camera switched over to the adopted mother's mailbox and the name on the mailbox was the Harrison's, how ironic.

I was older when I lived with the Harrison's and remembered much more than I could remember when living with the prior foster homes. One thing I do remember clearly was that Mr. and Mrs. Harrison were supposed to legally adopt my sister and me, but it never happened and I never found out why.

"Chores at the Harrison's"

We did more than our share of chores we washed the dishes, cleaned the bathrooms, made beds, and dusted the furniture. They had a large finished basement where all the meals were eaten and it had a tile floor. Every Saturday was general cleaning, so my sister and I would go on our hands and knees and Brillo the entire tile floor. Of course this taught us how to clean, but come on, we did too much.

Their yard was beautiful, but it was full of weeds and we had to do all the weeding. I hated it. They had a daughter and son, and they treated us like family, but when it came to shoveling the snow out of their long driveway, we did it, not their daughter or son. They had a big back yard consisting of a raspberry orchard, which my sister and I picked each morning to add to our cereal. We also collected lightning bugs that would fly amongst the raspberry bushes in the evening. We would put them in jars and see the jar light up.

In their finished basement, they had a monkey named Chipsey. He was kept in a cage in the fireplace where wood would go. Every day, it was one of my chores to clean the cage, and I will never forget the distinct odor that came from that cage. Before I cleaned it, I had to let Chipsey out, and as I did, he managed to bite my finger, and blood was gushing from my finger. I was in agony no one came to my rescue. I put a towel around it and continued cleaning the cage and put Chipsey back and tended to my wound, even though I was in pain I still loved Chipsey, he did not mean to bite me.

We played a lot at the Harrison's, with a ball in the street, with friends, and with baby dolls until the Harrison's daughter had twins and we helped take care of them. We never had Barbie dolls like other girls had at our age, so when we went to our friend's house, we played with hers. We also listened to records on her record player and danced. This was something we never were allowed to do before.

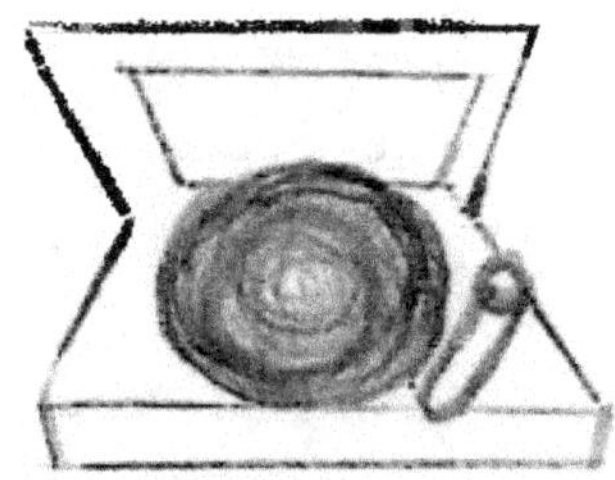

The Harrison's son joined the Navy, and while there, he brought our pictures with him and showed them to all of his Navy buddies, telling them that we were his sisters. He did not show a picture of his real sister, and I felt bad but could not hide the pride and happiness I felt, too. He would be gone for months at a time, but when he came home, it was always a surprise he would come in and slam his duffle bag on the floor and everyone would run to welcome him home.

Their daughter was much older than us and was always nice to us. I do not remember much about her except that she, like her mom, wore starched dresses. I never saw them wear anything else. They both would iron everything with starch, even their handkerchiefs. She wore her hair really short just like Mr. Harrison wanted our hair to be worn. Her friends would come over and play records in their basement, and I would hang around them. I was fourteen at the time. All her friends thought I was ten years old. I was so upset. I hated looking so young for my age, but today it is beneficial to me.

Mr. Harrison had a very bad temper, which affected me later on in life. I was afraid of any man with a temper, and I suffer from PTSD because of it. Another foster child lived with us, and he was around five years old. When he got in trouble, Mr. Harrison would kick him into a cabinet in the basement for punishment.

During our time at the Harrisons, our mom would still come on a monthly basis to take us out for the day. She had the same song and dance that she would take us back as soon as she married again, but the visits became less and less. We still always had in the back of our minds that someday in the near future she would come and take us home to our tiny house.

On one of our visits to our mom's tiny house, I remember taking my little brother, who was only two at the time and I was only six, for a walk in his stroller to a deli that was quite a distance from the house. I was surprised my mom let us go, being so little, but I forgot she never cared anyway. On our stroll to the deli, we passed a long row of daffodils a long side a garage, and they were beautiful. I will always remember that walk with my brother and the daffodils, which is one of my favorite flowers today.

"Real Mom"

I really contradict myself when I call my biological mom my mom; the truth is I loved my Harrison mom. It takes more than giving birth to a child to be a mom. I just finished my photo albums. I have several pictures of my biological mom. I say to myself, "Does she deserve even being in my album? Not really." I thought about it and decided to put her in there only because she gave me life and that is all, she is part of my history. Of course, I have a picture of Mrs. Harrison in my album.

Later on in my life, Mrs. Harrison was hospitalized and I had not seen her for a while. I went up to her bedside and told her I loved her. This was not easy, because of the lack of I love I always had, but I found the courage to do so and I am so happy I did.

I have a picture of my twin sister and me. My sister had a smile on her face and I had a sad face. I feel so bad for those two beautiful three-year-old little girls, given away so young and no family to step in and raise them. Where was my mom when I was sick, when I cried or got hurt? Mrs. Harrison was there and she would buy us crayons and coloring books when we got sick. One time I faked being sick just so I could get the crayons and coloring book.

My mom kept my three brothers and raised them, but she did not keep us because we would be too much competition for her as we got older. I am sure my brothers had love for her, but they probably also had unpleasant moments.

"School at the Harrisons"

My sister and I attended high school, and back then it started at ninth grade. We did not enjoy school too much because we never dressed like the other girls. We wore saddle shoes, knee socks, and had really short hair, and the other girls wore stockings with white polished sneakers, a style back then. We never had store bought clothes. Mr. Harrison drove a delivery truck for a drycleaner and brought clothes home that customers left behind.

They were not new, but I loved them, I remember a sailor outfit with a pleated skirt was my favorite. The shoes we wore were new, but we were not allowed to pick out any we liked. We had brown shoes with tassels on them which smelled brand new. I loved the smell, just like the first week of school with the smell of new books and a new school bag. We always brought lunch to school and never were able to buy hot lunch, which I craved. The lunchroom offered ice cream for a dime, but we never had a dime, so we always tried grubbing a dime off our friends.

Mr. Harrison always lectured us that we were not in school to attract boys, we were there to learn. Feeling like outcasts was all that was on our minds. If we would have dressed like the other girls, we would have done better in school. It did not help that I had this mad crush on a boy named Bobby, and he never even noticed me.

In school, I always wanted to be someone else. I would copy how another girl would walk and I would walk that way. I would copy someone else's handwriting and write that way. I could never be myself I think because I was never accepted for being myself, but after high school, I realized that I am who I am and I would have to be liked for me, not anyone else.

We always had in our minds that we were not worthy of love and if we were someone else, maybe we would be. As I got older, I would look for love in all the wrong places and never knew how to accept love. I never believed I deserved it, and I never knew what real love was until later on in my life.

One day at school, I found out that the music teacher was auditioning a male and female jazz singer for the high school jazz band so I auditioned. I sang "Rocking Around the Christmas Tree" with such energy, and I was chosen amongst the entire high school. We performed at a concert in the auditorium of the high school. I was so nervous my knees were shaking but when I saw Mrs. Harrison in the audience, I felt so much better. This was one of the highlights of high school. The other was typing and shorthand, both of which I excelled in. One of my childish dreams was to become a secretary someday, and I succeeded to be a secretary and administrative assistant.

"Never to Go Home Again"

It seemed hopeless that we would ever go home and live with our mom again. She always promised to marry and take us back. The worst part of not going back was lacking the closeness with our three brothers. We loved them but it would have been better if we grew up together in the same home. We were actually shunned by all of our natural family and it's still like that today. It is like we are the bad ones, and we gave ourselves up to child welfare. Meanwhile, it was our mom who gave us up and never took us back.

The very few times we did have a once a month visit with our mom, she told us to tell everyone, especially any men folk she was entertaining, who would not think too highly of her knowing about her lie, that we were her nieces, because she did not want to reveal the truth. She was never proud and never will be proud of having beautiful twin daughters. How could I expect her to be proud of her grandchildren? she was not even proud of her daughters. Uncle Jay was the only one in the family, at that time, that was proud of us.

"Frightful Mr. Harrison"

The only downfall living with the Harrisons was that Mr. Harrison had a bad temper and it made me terrified, so my sister and I would hide anytime he started with his temper. My sister and I slept upstairs, and we would wait on the steps for Mr. Harrison to come and kiss us goodnight, because we all kissed good morning and goodnight at the Harrison's house. Each time he kissed us, he told us to pucker up our lips and we went along with it, what did we know? Another time, Mr. Harrison had a few drinks and he was outside, so I went to kiss him goodnight, like any normal night before I went to bed. He picked me up and straddled me around his waist. I could smell the liquor on his breath as I proceeded to kiss him, and he put his tongue in my mouth. I did not know what was happening, I thought it was normal.

The next morning, I went down to join everyone for breakfast and kissed Mr. Harrison good morning and put my tongue in his mouth, like he did to me the night before. Much to my surprise, he smacked me in the mouth and gave me a bloody lip. I was so shocked and confused, but I realized later he had to put on a show as to not let Mrs. Harrison find out what he did. This situation only added to the terrible nightmares I already had.

I never remember Mr. Harrison's son ever being disrespectful to his parents. One day, I was sitting on the patio and saw Mr. Harrison grab his son in a choke hold and wrestle him to the ground. The son was an adult. Why did his father do this? Maybe the son said something the father did not agree with, but that does not call for that kind of abuse from his father, it was so sad to witness the abuse; he was such a good son. Not too long after that incident, the son made a career of the Navy and while there, he met a young lady and was married. He moved not too far from his parents.

"The Neighbor"

There was a very nice neighbor, or so I thought, who lived across from the Harrisons house. I was outside in the front, and he waived to me to come over. I was not hesitant because the Harrisons were good friends with him. He wanted me to come in the house to show me around, and no one else was home at the time so I went in. He showed me all the rooms downstairs and took me to the upstairs bedrooms.

He walked over to one of the beds and asked me to feel how soft the mattress was so I went over and sat on it. All of a sudden, he bent down and tried to kiss me. All can remember is that I pushed his hairy unclothed upper body off of me and ran out of the house as fast as my feet could carry me. I told the Harrisons what he did and they did nothing, life went on as usual. I felt horrified when I went home to think that a neighbor and good friend of the Harrison's would do that.

There were many nights I could not go to sleep for fear of the nightmares I had of his hairy chest coming down on me. The neighbor knew I was a foster child and took full advantage of that, thinking no one would do anything and no one did. Since that had happened, I was always afraid to go in the front yard for fear that he would approach me. The few times that I had to, he would be on his front porch staring at me. I was so frightened and could not tell anyone because it was a waste of time, they would not do anything anyway.

Why would a social worker from child welfare have us live with families that are abusive? When we moved to different foster homes, there was never a second visit from the social worker to see if we were okay. The only way they knew that something was wrong was complaints from the neighbors. What kind of system was this? We should have had advocates fighting for us. I sure hope it is different today.

"Seventeen and Boys"

Life at the Harrisons went on, and now my sister and I were seventeen. When a boy at school asked you to the movies back then, it meant it was make out time. Well, Vinnie, who I went to school with, asked me to the movies and I said yes. As we sat watching the movie, Vinnie put his arm around me and touched my elbow and said, "You have really soft elbows." It never went any further, his dad drove me home, and Vinnie walked me to the door then kissed me on my cheek. He then commented if that did not happen, he would not take me out again and he never did. I could not have cared less.

My very first boyfriend was Jerry. He was the cousin of my friend that lived down the block from me, and her name was Julie. Julie always stood out because she had natural frosted hair and I wanted it so bad, today, my hair is frosted because of her. Jerry always walked to my house, and we would watch television or play cards. At this time, the Four Seasons just came out and my favorite song was Sherry because every time I heard it, I would say Jerry instead. I learned as I went on hanging out with Jerry that he really admired himself. He gave me two 8 x 10 colored photographs of himself that I kept long after we broke up.

Then there was Billy; he was a junior football player. I watched all his games and was proud I was going out with a football player. He was really nice. He took me to meet his parents, and I did the same with him and the Harrisons. We actually did kiss and everything was proper, but the relationship did not last, it just faded out.

I started dating a college boy named Jimmy who I met at the beach one day. He had approached me, but I was nervous and surprised because he was a lifeguard and he wanted to date me. I was so excited to be a lifeguard's girl. The Harrisons liked Jimmy a lot because he was in college and Jimmy's mom liked me, too. Jimmy's mom gave me a beautiful green dress with black polka dots to wear to my concert. Jimmy gave me his pin from college and I was pinned, whatever that meant. He really liked me, and I liked him.

Dating can be hard to deal with, but luckily we had Mrs. Harrison to turn to if we had an issue. My biological mom was out of site and not seen for a long while. She went on with her life with my brothers and never even called us for our birthdays, but of course, we had a good birthday with Mrs. Harrison. Our mom's words never left us that she would marry someday and take us back to live with her.

We wanted to be loved and noticed by her just like at the end of a movie where a mom and children are reunited. Unfortunately, my life is not a movie. Speaking of movies, as I got older, I would call my mom and she would be in the middle of watching a television show and did not want to be interrupted by her daughter. Guess what the show was? It was "Highway to Heaven." How could she watch that when she never had a heavenly bone in her body, at least I never felt it.

I tried to build some kind of relationship with her after all those years, but it seemed impossible. What a hypocrite to watch such a godly show and treat you daughter the way she did. I called many times and received the same response, so I finally gave up. Today or any day, when one of my children call me, I stop whatever I am doing and take the call because they come first before anything, unless I am in the shower or cannot get to the phone, then I would call them back as soon as I was able. The main reason I have a phone was for my family to reach me which is the most important thing for me.

I am a role model for my children I put them before anyone. I am the mother my mom never was and could never be. They have hugs and kisses all the time and know they are loved unconditionally.

"The Large Family"

Life went on, and while I was still dating Jimmy a large family moved from Brooklyn into the corner house on our block. They had fourteen children, who I thought some were adopted, but that was not so. One day, I walked past their house, saw a teenage girl outside, and started talking to her. Silly me, I asked her if she had any older brothers. I was curious and she said yes, she had two. This family was pure Italian, and I am a mixture of Scottish, Irish, French, and German. I always wanted to be Italian because the girls would mature faster, have olive skin, and black hair. Of course, I always wanted to be someone else, so that was obvious.

The next day, I went back over to the corner house and met the younger of the two older brothers, Jerry. We would hang out and play ball outside almost daily. But when I met the older brother Lenny, I immediately fell head over heels in love, at least what I thought was love at seventeen. He did not know I was alive. Lenny was from Brooklyn and was used to tough girls, and when he moved to Long Island he had to break up with his Brooklyn girlfriend.

Before I met Lenny in person, I would look out my bedroom window and watch the corner house where he lived. One day, Lenny took a walk down the block. I will never forget; he had a blue mohair sweater on and had a bop when he walked. He had black hair, and he reminded me of John Travolta walking down the street in "Saturday Night Fever."

Lenny's sister gave me a picture of Lenny, and I showed all my friends at school. I knew that Lenny liked tough Brooklyn girls, so when I went over there I tried to act tough, but I should have just been myself. Lenny played the drums really well and played them while listening to records in his basement as he dreamed of the Brooklyn girl he left behind.

One day, Lenny, Jerry, their sisters, and I walked to a small house party not far from Lenny's house. On the way, Lenny came next to me and said he would take care of me later, but then later never came. On one occasion, I was over Lenny's and he noticed me as I was sitting on his living room couch. He whispered in my ear, "Come back later without your bra and girdle." I never heard such a thing; it went in one ear out the other. Like I said earlier, he was used to Brooklyn girls and not a girl like me.

Lenny's family was great and welcoming. All the girls cleaned together and had fun doing it. When they were not cleaning, they would be dancing and I danced with them like I never did before. I loved hearing them talk they talked so much. They had special dinners like macaroni and meatballs and all sorts of delicious Italian meals. I ate over a couple of times; it was unbelievable.

I went down in their basement one day, and Lenny kissed me. I was elated and in heaven, I thought it was unbelievable. The next morning, his sister told me, "My brother does not like you because you kiss like a wall." I was devastated. I went home and cried myself to sleep. Falling so hard for Lenny helped me get over Bobby, who I had a mad crush on in school.

"Run"

The next day was Sunday, and my sister and I and the Harrisons were having Sunday breakfast together. While eating, Mr. Harrison started talking about the night before. He knew I was at Lenny's, and he and Mrs. Harrison were there also playing cards with Lenny's family. He said he did not want me going over Lenny's anymore, and this really shook me up. I had the most fun with their family, and Mr. Harrison wanted to put an end to it. To think of it today, he probably wanted to save me for himself because of his prior sexual advances toward me.

All I could do was sit quiet and listen as he went on talking, and he said to Mrs. Harrison, "We will have her hair cut really short, like we had done when she was younger." My hair was finally long at seventeen, and I loved it. How could he be so cruel? All because he was jealous I was having so much fun over Lenny's, and he knew how I felt about Lenny.

My sister and I finished eating and proceeded to the kitchen to do the dishes as we always did. Mr. and Mrs. Harrison were still talking about the incident over and over again. Mom Harrison said, "We could put her in a girl's home." I could not understand why and I said yes because I was so frightened that Mr. Harrison's temper would flare. At that moment, Mom Harrison said, "I wish I was dead," for what reason is beyond me. That was all Mr. Harrison had to hear. His temper flared and he looked so scary and evil. I was so terrified.

I had the feeling of running away from this awful situation and was so sad I may never see Lenny again. How could I, where would I go? At that moment Mr. Harrison jumped off his chair and proceeded to come after me, my blouse tore as he grabbed me. I was able to free myself and grab my sister's hand and run as fast as I could out of the house down the block.

As I approached Lenny's house, his sister was outside and asked what was wrong, she saw my torn blouse and noticed I was really upset. I told her what had happened and how frightened I was and she said, "Come in, I will hide you guys in my bedroom so my parents will not see you when they return home." I remember having a dish of pasta fagioli for the first time, and we ate it on a suit case in her bedroom. I will never forget, it was delicious, one of their many Italian meals.

Lenny's sister said we had to hide in the basement because her mom and dad were coming home and she did not want to get in trouble. So, we hid downstairs by the washing machine where clothes were on the floor to be washed.

I realized we could not stay there much longer. We left and ran down the street again, paranoid of somebody behind us. We hid behind bushes and trees and it became really dark and more frightful. There was a boy I went to school with who lived not too far from where we were running. I knocked on his door and told his mom the situation, and she called the police.

"Going Home To Our Mom"

I told the police what had happened and how frightened we were of Mr. Harrison and how he tore my blouse. I said I wanted to go to my real mom's house. Of course, it was never the intention to go back in this way. I always wanted it to be my mom's decision, but it never was.

My mom lived with one of my brothers, one was in the service, and my older brother was married. When we got to our mom's house, she took us in but did not seem too happy about it. We had no choice, where would we go, we have not lived with her since we were five years old, and now we were seventeen.

My mom did not live in the tiny house anymore, she rented a bigger house consisting of a living room, large dining room, an eat in kitchen, two bedrooms, and an indoor bathroom. My mom had one bedroom and my brother had the other one, which had a full-size bed and twin bed, and the living room had a sofa bed, which my sister slept on.

Unfortunately, I slept on a plastic weaved lawn chair right next to the empty twin bed. This is something I will never forget; how could she do this? I just did not know how to feel sleeping on that lawn chair, I could hardly sleep it was so uncomfortable, but my mom only worried about me making noise and her waking up. I was somewhat grateful to have a place to sleep and a roof over my head, but that was all. I did not want to upset her for any reason and be out on the street.

Being a mom myself, I could never imagine having my child sleep on a lawn chair by any means. What was she thinking or did she even think? I know my grandmother was very cold, my mom's mother, but this is no reason for my mom to be that way. You do not want your children to go through what you went through as a child, so you do the best to avoid it. As far as jealousy, how can a mom be jealous of her own flesh and blood? I am so proud of my beautiful children, because I am a real mom, not her.

A couple of days after the move, the social worker notified me that she would get all my clothes and personal items from the Harrisons for me. Mr. Harrison gathered up all my belongings, so I thought, and gave them to the social worker to bring to me. When I received them, it was such a small amount of clothes and no personal items. I was missing Jerry's pictures and most important of all, a folder of pictures from the movie King of Kings which were so dear to me.

My sister and I would go to the movies on the weekend, and one of the movies I most remember was King of Kings. It really made an impression on me. Jeffrey Hunter starred as Jesus, the best portrayal I have ever seen. My favorite scene was when Jesus was baptized and he arose from the water and all you could see were his deep blue eyes and his wet hair dangling to his shoulders. I came out of the theatre that day feeling so holy and spiritual it made me want to be a nun someday.

Soon after my sister went back to live with the Harrisons because she could not take living with my mom any longer. Who could blame her? We would have to be on tip toes not to wake her in the morning, and I would have to lie in the lawn chair until she woke up. She also made sure we were never around when she had men visitors. She was jealous of our youth and beauty; she was afraid we would interfere with her visitor.

"New Girl"

While living with my mom, I started school at Bay Shore High and I was the new girl. After my years at the Harrison's when I was an outcast, I was finally not one anymore. I dressed so cute with a straight skirt, little heels, and my hair long with a little poof on top and no makeup at all.

Everyone noticed me when I walked down the hall, even the teachers. I could not believe it. What a wonderful feeling, unlike the feeling living with the Harrisons. If Bobby, who I had a mad crush on, would have seen me now as a new girl like everyone else saw me, maybe he would have given me a first and even second look, but I would never have given up Lenny for Bobby. I really liked this school, I was in regent classes, business courses, and I received an award for shorthand. I was really adjusting to my new life in my new school.

Soon after I received a big surprise. Lenny decided to visit me. He walked from West Babylon all the way to Bay Shore, to see me. I guess he liked me now so we started hanging out, I was so happy. The way I felt about Lenny made me totally forget about Jimmy, but Jimmy did not forget about me. He started dating Lenny's sister just to be close to me and get me back. When I think about it, I feel bad because we went to the drive-in movies together with Jimmy and

Lenny's sister in front and Lenny and I in the back. It was sad, but my feelings were for Lenny.

As I was walking to school one day, a man approached me and gave me his card. He was from Harper's Bazar magazine and he wanted me to model for him. I was not sure if it was on the up and up, so when I got home, I gave my older brother the card and he called and found out that it was legit. Lenny was jealous that I was going to model and without independence of my own, I listened to Lenny and did not proceed with this opportunity.

I was happy going to school, but it did not last long. My mother kept getting mad at me for waking her up when I got ready for school each morning. One day, she had enough and went to the high school and signed me out and there was no advocate there to fight for me. Later on in life I was able to get my GED, but it was not the same, though.

"Lenny's Aunt"

When my mother signed me out of school, it put the icing on the cake. I was a fool to even want to live with her, what a mistake! She was so selfish; she only thought of what was good for her and she did not care how leaving school would affect my future.

It turns out Lenny's Aunt Amy moved to Deer Park Long Island with her small daughter and her two sons, Lenny's cousins. She needed a live-in babysitter and housecleaner. It was an opportunity for me, not the best, but the only one I had.

Living at Lenny's Aunt Amy's was not what I expected, I was, however, grateful to have a roof over my head and still be able to date Lenny. One cousin was Lenny's age and the other was older. They all went to work daily, and I stayed home to babysit and clean the house as arranged. There was drama every night when they came home. Aunt Amy would argue with the younger of the two cousins. It was very loud and disruptive, not what I bargained for, not a good atmosphere for anyone, but there was nothing I could do I had nowhere to go.

One day, the older cousin stayed home from work and decided to chase me all over the house to try and kiss me, even though he knew I was dating Lenny. He proceeded to drag me to the bedroom where he threw me on the bed and hung my head off the edge of the bed, so I would give up and kiss him, but I broke free. He then realized he had no chance at all.

I think when the family lived in Brooklyn, they shared girlfriends, but they were not in Brooklyn anymore. When I saw Lenny that evening, I told him what had transpired. He was really upset and confronted his cousin and it never happened again. Will I ever be free of people trying to abuse me?

Not too long after, my sister needed a place to stay, she had enough with the Harrisons, finally. So, Aunt Amy decided she can move in, but she would have to go to work to pay for her room and board. It was good having my sister live with me again, but Aunt Amy was awful and moody. She would like one of us one day, and then not the next, nothing ever ran smoothly. I guess it is just the way life goes.

After my sister had enough living at Lenny's aunt's house, she moved in with Mr. Harrison's son and wife. Through all my experiences as a foster child, I did not let it ruin my future. I will always regret not having the love as a child that I should have had, because it does affect your entire life. I never let it come between myself and my children.

My sister and I were certainly lost in the welfare system, and when I think back it always makes me sad and angry to know how the system failed us. I watch a lot of television movies about foster children being bounced from one home to another but always a happy ending, and I always wished that I was in their shoes. In the movie, the social worker was so involved with the care of the foster children, she visited them in their new home several times to make sure they were taken care of properly, but not in our case, like I said earlier our life was not like a movie, unfortunately for us.

Years went by and I received a call from my family that my mom had passed away. She had been in the hospital for a while but no one even called us because we were still outcasts as far as they were concerned. I went to the wake and stayed a short while because this was all the respect she deserved. I never dwelled on the past. Although by writing my story, it brought up bad memories that are haunting me right now. I say to myself why this or why that, but I have to let it go for my own sanity. Often, I felt like nobody, but I found out that God never made a nobody, only a somebody.

"The Future"

I was eighteen and still living with Lenny's Aunt Amy while continuing to date Lenny. I saw Lenny almost every night. His dad would visit Aunt Amy every night so Lenny tagged along to see me. Lenny was getting his license soon. During the day I would work in a dress shop along with Aunt Amy and Lenny which was great because we had a ride to work with Aunt Amy. One day at work and I felt so sick and could not figure out why. I soon figured it out I was pregnant and so scared someone would find out.

It was very hard not to give in to Lenny's desires because of how I felt about him and it did not help that he was very hard to resist with his black hair, olive skin, and that Italian demeanor. I knew this from the very beginning. At this time, I was turning nineteen and Lenny eighteen looking back we were just too young. Lenny went home that night and told his parents, they were shocked but said they would support us in any way they could.

They said that I could move in with them so I was not afraid to tell Aunt Amy, because I had another place to go. I moved in but slept in a different room than Lenny until we got married. His parents planned for us to marry very soon. It is not like today where you can walk around pregnant and not be married; all eyes would be on you.

The Harrisons were told by my sister, and they offered to be witnesses when we were married. The night before I was to marry Lenny, the Harrisons let me sleep at their house because the groom is not to see the bride before the wedding. The next morning, Lenny's parents, the Harrisons, and I all went to the church. I was so nervous. The church was in Deer Park a cute little white church with a red carpet where we were married, and it was a beautiful little ceremony.

Lenny and I never had a chance to have a honeymoon, so Lenny's parents had a reception down in their basement and set up a bedroom upstairs in their home for us. I was very happy to finally have Lenny all to myself, but embarrassed in front of any family members that would visit, knowing I had to get married because I was pregnant. It took me a long time to feel better about this.

Life went on with Lenny, and soon I gave birth to a beautiful baby girl. It was so unbelievable. Lenny went to work and I stayed home at Lenny's parent's house to care for our daughter. Months went by until we finally could afford our own apartment, it was a challenge, but we made it work. As time went on in our tiny three-room apartment, I realized I was pregnant again, and nine months later, I gave birth to another beautiful daughter.

Unfortunately, the welfare department was never out of my life totally. Times were hard and Lenny worked very hard, but it still was not enough to support our growing family so we had to get supplemental help from social services, which I was embarrassed about, but also grateful for the help.

My family and I moved so many times, every time we rented a house it was time to move again, it was put up for sale. My son's friend would ask him, "Are you moving? It has been two years." This was true because it happened every two years. My kids had to change schools and leave their friends, not something we had control over, we just did not have enough money to buy our own house. I always said that I never had any roots just like the movie, because I moved around since I was five and it never ended.

I went on to have three more daughters and two sons. It was a really full house you could say. Once my youngest turned five and went off to school, I went to work and vowed never to go on social services again and I never did. My first job was in a button factory, and now we had two paychecks, which really helped our living situation. The craziest thing about me working in a button factory is that I found out recently it was my mom's first job, which is unbelievable.

During the time of caring for my children and working in the button factory, Lenny decided to take karate lessons, which he went almost every night after work. After a long time, he achieved his black belt and went on to an even higher belt- fifth degree. He taught classes in the school he was attending and also went to tournaments until one day he was able to open his own school.

He had so many students young and old; they learned self-defense for the street and they were not to let anyone know about what they learned, because it was an ultimate surprise for any attacker. Our sons and a few of our daughters also attended the school. Lenny had his karate school for twenty-five years and finally closed the doors due to his retirement and not feeling well.

As my children grew up to be adults themselves, they moved on, some married, some stayed single, but they always came to see us. Now that my children were off on their own, I got a position further from home as an administrative assistant in a CPA firm and also became a realtor. With my salary and Lenny's, we were able to establish good credit and buy our first home and then we would not have to move again, hopefully. I feel bad we were not able to buy it when our children were young, but they were still very happy for us.

I know I had said that hopefully we would never have to move again but I had to think of Lenny's and my future when we retired. My eldest daughter recently moved upstate, so we took a trip to visit her. During the visit I sat on her front porch and it felt so peaceful, no noise, not much traffic, so I had a brainstorm that we should move here.

So, on Thanksgiving, I took a trip there with one of my grandsons to look at homes for sale. The realtor took us around several neighborhoods to view homes, and as we passed a gray two-family house with a porch, I was sold. The home was a two family, just perfect for us, with the second-floor apartment, it would be extra income to make the mortgage, along with Lenny's social security and the job I would get.

Before the move, Lenny's big toe turned black due to an infection from diabetes, so the doctors decided to amputate it. While in the hospital after the toe was removed, Lenny said, "I gave the black toe to the black guy in the next bed." Lenny was a real jokester.

I never figured out why Lenny turned out to be the unhealthy one of his entire family, he was the best of the bunch, always there for everyone especially his mom. I know that the three and a half packs of cigarettes he smoked daily did not help. At the age of forty-two, Lenny had open heart surgery and before going into surgery, he went into the hospital bathroom and smoked, but after surgery, he finally quit.

Lenny always seemed indestructible until he would get attacks of his heart beating fast for many years and had to go to the hospital, but he never wanted to stay. His words were "Heaven can wait." Finally, one day after several ambulance trips to the hospital, he decided to stay. The doctors found that he had scar tissue in the middle of his chest, which caused these attacks, so they performed an ablation, and it solved the problem.

Finally, it was time for Lenny and me to make the move upstate to our home we had purchased. It was hard leaving our children that still lived on Long Island, but they visited us and we visited them when possible. Lenny had retired earlier and I continued to work. My eldest daughter lived upstate with my grandson, grand-godson, and a couple of Lenny's sisters, which made us happy to have family nearby. I found a job in a lawyer's office not too far from where we lived.

We enjoyed living upstate, we worked on the house, and Lenny let me pick out whatever colors I wanted to paint and never once complained that they were too girlish, even though they were. College girls rented the second-floor apartment but eventually moved out, and my younger daughter, my small grandchild, and her husband moved in.

Within the first year of living in our new home, I continued working and Lenny completed tasks around the house. During this time, Lenny started feeling sick all the time from his diabetes, his foot where his toe was removed became infected and he had to be hospitalized and was sent home a few days later with antibiotics. A wound care nurse came to our house once a week to address the wound, but the infection was not getting any better so he had to be hospitalized again. Lenny was in and out of the hospital too many times so I decided to retire to be with him constantly, and I was by his side for his entire time in the hospital, only going home at night, because there was no way you could sleep in the hospital with lights on, nurses in and out. I needed my rest to be there for Lenny.

I noticed other wives visited their husbands or loved ones, and they left after a short visit I thought it was sad that their loved ones would be gone for such a long time. A lot of family came and visited from time to time and it helped having them there. The doctors tried every kind of antibiotic to heal Lenny's infection, which had turned septic and spread to below his knee, but nothing seemed to work so he slipped into a coma. The doctors came to me and said that Lenny was dying because not too many people survived septic infections. I did not listen to the doctor. I let it go in one ear and out the other. I knew in my heart this could not be true.

While Lenny was in a coma, my daughter brought a small radio with a CD player in it and played 50s music alongside his bed. One day when I was by his bedside, along with my daughter, Lenny started singing a few lyrics of a 50s song with his eyes still closed, it was unbelievable. A couple of days later, Lenny came out of his coma and said he had seen his mom and dad. They told him it was not his time yet, so go back.

Soon, his infection looked like it was healing and Lenny felt a little better and sat in the recliner next to his bed along with his urine bag attached. I happened to look at his belly; it looked so bloated and his urine bag only had a drop of urine in it. I buzzed for the nurse to get the doctor so I could find out what was going on. Due to all the antibiotics, Lenny's kidneys had failed and he needed daily dialysis to survive. The doctors were not going to give him dialysis because he still had an infection, but I insisted, because otherwise Lenny would have died. Without dialysis to take out the urine which the body could not release on its own, his system would have been poisoned.

"Caregiver"

Lenny finally came home to be cared for by a wound care nurse that came twice a week to address the rest of the infection, and we also had to visit the doctor once a month to check the wound. The news was not good; the doctor said his infection was not going away and the leg below the knee would have to be amputated. What devastating news, but we did not have a choice because the infection would have traveled even further up his leg. The day came for the surgery, Lenny stayed in the hospital for quite a while, and I was right by his side the entire time.

The times in the hospital were exhausting, and more than once I had to speak to the manager of the hospital to address situations by the nursing staff. It has always been said that the squeaky wheel gets the grease, well I was that squeaky wheel, Lenny's advocate.

I mentioned earlier that Lenny has always been indestructible. In the forty-seven years I have been his wife, this man has been through more than any human being that I have known, having had diabetes, coronary artery disease, heart failure, a defibrillator placed near his heart, and amputation. With all the pain he suffered, he never ever complained; he had courage beyond courage. Later in this story you will read Lenny's story from his own words written down by a social worker that visited Lenny once a week at his bedside.

Months went by and Lenny's other leg below the knee became infected at this time and also had to be amputated. Lenny was receiving long term care at home instead of going in a nursing home, and I was his long-time caregiver. Being a caregiver, you do not have much time for yourself. I only was able to shower twice a week when in normal week, it would be daily.

During this time, I would sit alongside Lenny's bedside and crochet, filling two large bins. At this time, the hospital wanted me to put Lenny on hospice and I said, "No way, as long as he is breathing, I will take care of him." I did it and would have for the rest of my life if I had to. Lenny had a motorized wheel chair to get around the house in and also managed to go on our front porch to see the sights. There was no way he could have gone in the backyard until my son came and built him a ramp with a deck in two days. Lenny also had two prosthetics that helped him take a few steps with the help of physical therapy once a week.

Lenny had dialysis twice a week, and we were blessed to have the coverage for a hospital medivan to pick him up and bring him to dialysis and home twice a week. I also had a hospital bed, table, oxygen tank, and commode. Lenny came home so weak from his dialysis and went straight into his bedroom sitting up, waiting for me to make him a special breakfast, then he would fall fast asleep.

We had an aid come twice a week for two hours, which made it possible for me to run errands. The aid would wash Lenny the best she could, but I washed him with love, which was so much better. A nurse came twice a week to see how he was doing, checking his vitals, wounds, and his mental health. She was a great nurse, very dedicated to her patient. I loved her. I knew she really cared for Lenny.

As Lenny's caregiver and his wife, I was depressed a lot seeing him in this condition twenty-four hours a day. It was really tough to deal with, but what does not kill you makes you stronger, I have heard. The biggest thing of all is that God got me through it, God does not make things happen in life unless he is there to guide you through them.

I do not like writing this but I have to, after three and a half years of caring for Lenny, God had called him home. This was the most devastating time of our lives. Life went on for us, I do not know how, but it did. Lenny had told my eldest daughter in confidence, "Please watch out for your mother, I want her to go on living. I do not want anyone to hurt her in any way." Life does go on and you can love again but never the same. During Lenny's illnesses, we lost our homes, but nothing compared to losing Lenny.

You have heard my story in my words, now it is time for Lenny's story in his words, coming up in the next chapter to give other people in Lenny's shoes, the courage to go on like Lenny did. The story was dictated word for word by Lenny to a social worker that visited Lenny once a week. The social worker would sit by Lenny's bedside and write down Lenny's words as he spoke.

"Lenny's Story"

Lenny Jr. born October, 1947 in Brooklyn, New York, one of many children born to his parents. Lenny was the oldest of six boys, and two older sisters and six younger sisters. Lenny had a brother who was a year or so younger than him that he was always protective of. "I never let anybody mess with him," said Lenny.

When Lenny was age six or seven, he accompanied his brother, then age five, for two weeks to Camp McDonald, a Catholic summer camp for children on Long Island. The two boys traveled by bus from Brooklyn to the camp. Along the way, an older boy on the bus started messing with his brother. In response, Lenny told the guy, "Hey, when this bus stops, you stop breathing." When the bus stopped, Lenny kept his promise without interference from anyone. "In the 50s, you gave the beating and it was over, not like today. Today it's the peace sign, and 'I will sue you'," said Lenny.

Once they arrived at Camp McDonald, was it a pleasant experience for the boys? "It was supposed to be," said Lenny with a scowl. The boys slept in a long line of bunks in a barracks setting with a code of conduct that was strictly enforced by stern, strict nuns. "They used to swat our asses with our pants down, with a wooden paddle," Lenny recalled. "They would say, 'I do not like what you are doing,' and they would swat us."

Lenny also remembered wondering what was happening to those nuns at night because around midnight, Lenny would hear the nuns screaming loudly. "But in the morning, they woke up nice and fresh," he said.

The camp was in a wooded area and like a military base with four big long buildings as dormitories and a mess hall. There was a swimming pool, and the kids had to wear camp issued bathing suits that were made of an irritating fabric that to Lenny felt like coarse burlap. When Lenny was pushed to say something nice about the camp, he said that in the afternoon the kids got milk and donuts, he liked that.

Back in Brooklyn, Lenny played a lot of handball like most city kids and also enjoyed playing stick ball. At nighttime, he would go to the park to hang out with the crowd of his friends or hang around the candy store, just the way Fonzi lived, meaning Fonzi the popular character on the television series, "Happy Days," about American life in the 1950s.

Lenny started working at the age of nine shining shoes, and he continued to be the protector of his family on the mean city streets. He remembered the time when he was thirteen at his home in the two-family house they lived in Brooklyn and someone had informed him one of his sisters had been hit by a boy waiting for the bus.

"I did fifty-two steps of stairs within ten seconds," said Lenny. Then, he sprinted the thirteen blocks to the bus stop he arrived just as the bus did. His sister pointed to a young man with a Hasidic Jew hair style and clothing who was entering the bus and was putting his money in,. "That was as far as it went; I hit him twenty-five times," said Lenny.

Physical confrontation was a frequent occurrence in Lenny's life. "I remember my first day of high school," said Lenny "I fought seven guys on my knees folded up. All they could hit was my arms and my ribs, big deal," said Lenny,. "I was built like a brick shit-house anyway. It took me four years to catch up with those guys and I got all of them."

Lenny remembered more of the first day of school like it was yesterday, "Tt was in gym," Lenny said. "I will never forget it." A single boy smaller than Lenny was wising off, otherwise provoking Lenny to fight him, and Lenny asked the boy if he wanted to fight in the gym or outside. "Outside three o'clock," the boy replied.

So, at three o'clock Lenny showed up outside and the boy was there. Lenny said to the boy, along with seven of the boy's friends, "I did not know you were in a gang." The gang was called the Junior Rompers. After being unfairly defeated by this gang, Lenny vowed to get revenge one small step at a time, and he did just that. Lenny took his time knowing that the recipients of his punishment would suffer the mental torment of anticipation before Lenny finally collected the payment due from each one of them.

"I would say 'you are next, you little bastard,' and the guy would say, 'I did not do anything', 'oh, no you were there!' I told him." Lenny would let his target stew in fear and worry and finally would confront him dealing out Lenny's physical justice with a beating. Lenny would invite each boy to have the other gang members present for the fight, but the other gang members never showed up because each had learned that it was a bad idea to mess with Lenny ever again.

Protection became a way of life and a career for Lenny. Soon he began studying martial arts at age twenty-one, by age twenty-three he reached the level of third-degree black belt in karate. Lenny continued to teach karate at his own school for a total of twenty-five years. Lenny provided guidance to the lives of one thousand karate students, maybe more, over those years.

Lenny also had a creative side. In the 1950s and 60s, Lenny was the drummer of two different bands that played fifties music and rock 'n roll. When the bands would hold an amateur hour, Lenny's wife would get up and sing with them. Lenny had 470cc chopper motorcycle. "It was fast," he said.

Lenny was a Suffolk County Auxiliary Police officer for four and a half years and was trusted to carry a firearm. He was also a process server; he would officially serve an individual with a legal document and often produced a hostile reaction by the recipient. It was not uncommon for Lenny to suggest that the angry recipient not shoot the messenger. He also operated a snow plow, and one terrible winter storm on Long Island, with minimal visibility and being on foot at the time, he realized he was about to be hit by a car that was traveling about twenty miles per hour.

Just before impact, he stopped his breathing, tensed himself, took a hit, and rolled of the hood of the car. "That is what saved my ass," he recalled. "People get hurt because they panic, just take the hit and say I am alive, because I did not panic." Lenny said he used this technique a number of times like when he fell off a ladder and did not get hurt. His wife commented that he is like a cat and has nine lives, thank God, he is indestructible.

Lenny's relationship with his father was an extremely difficult one. He never told Lenny he loved him. "He just could not get the words out," said Lenny. "On his deathbed I was with him alone. I told him that I loved him for the first time and the heart rhythm machines went crazy." Lenny said he never said he loved him, he learned to hold his feelings in from his father. Lenny's mom never said she loved you, but you knew she did, you just felt it.

Lenny had a strong memory of when he was seventeen he had purchased an old blue and white 1957 Mercury from an elderly man in nearby Hicksville. The car had not been running for quite some time, but it was in great condition with low mileage, somehow Lenny got it started he was thrilled.

One day, Lenny's father took the car away saying he was going to fix it, and that was the last time Lenny saw the car and his father never mentioned what he did with it. Lenny did not have any words for his father after that. Lenny went on working and on with his life, despite his difficult relationship with his father. Lenny enjoyed reminiscing about his younger days on the streets of Brooklyn, especially when the theme has to do with resilience in the face of adversity.

Lenny had the following memory about Christmas. It was in the early 1960s. Lenny and his wife resided in Babylon, Long Island with their four children at the time, the youngest was two. Lenny had been a presser in a dry cleaner that served a lot of customers, but he got laid off and out of work. It was Christmas week and there was no money to buy gifts.

Back then, the gas station would hand out plaid stamps to reward customers, purchases were redeemed at the plaid store in Brooklyn. Lenny did not realize that he had accumulated so many, and they were just tossed in his cluttered car, there were thousands of them. Lenny and his cousin gathered them all and cashed them in and the kids had a Christmas with presents, when Lenny spoke of this he had a smile on his face from ear to ear.

Lenny and his wife eventually would have seven children, and they all opened ten gifts each at Christmas time that Lenny and his wife watched with happiness. They never had extravagant gifts but they enjoyed ripping them all open with such excitement, which was something wonderful to watch as their parents.

Lenny once again recalled that his childhood relationship with his father had been extremely difficult. His father was not fond of working, so he sent his eldest children to work so they could hand over their paychecks to him at the end of the work week. Lenny accepted these painful memories and did not let them overwhelm him. At the same time, "I look up to her," he said, gesturing towards his wife and kids. He was a great father and husband.

Lenny recalled the days when he had two separate jobs as a presser, one for a Greek boss and one Italian boss. Despite Lenny's Italian heritage, the Italian employer was extremely cheap toward Lenny when it came to wages and benefits, even though Lenny had excellent skills and dedication to his work. Lenny threatened to quit the Italian employer if he did not give him a raise and one week's vacation. Lenny said, "You have to speak up, that is the only way you get respect," he then received a raise and a week's vacation.

Lenny's wife remembered that she and her twin sister at age five were removed from their mother due to her incompetence as a parent.

They spent the rest of their childhood in foster care. When his wife was age seventeen, she met Lenny, then only sixteen. To his wife, Lenny seemed much older with his mature streetwise demeanor, and Lenny had the looks of movie star John Travolta.

His wife sighed deeply as she described how "head over heels in love" she was for young Lenny. When the foster home his wife was living with protested her escalating romance with Lenny, she ran away from them and moved back with her mother until she and Lenny were married. Lenny and his wife have seven children, twenty-two grandchildren, and seven great grandchildren.

Throughout the many years they were together, his wife repeatedly demonstrated that her love for Lenny would never diminish, it would remain steadfast to the very end, and it did. During his last couple of years of life, Lenny befriended a social worker who had only a bit of karate training in his youth, but who had enough to appreciate the psychological benefits of it. The social worker greatly appreciated the opportunity to let Lenny explain the psychological elements of karate. The social worker listened carefully, capturing many of the gems of Lenny's wisdom and used his wisdom to benefit the social worker's clients. Lenny was happy when the social worker told him how others had benefited from his helpful wisdom.

The following is an uncompleted project Lenny hoped to publish as a self-help pamphlet to inspire others. Lenny envisioned that the cover of the pamphlet would have two photographs: one showing Lenny as a young black belt champion in the process of a leg kick and the other showing Lenny as a double amputee fighting a different kind of fight, but continuing to fight nonetheless. He wanted to title the pamphlet, "Finding Your Inner Courage and Strength," and he had hoped it would help its readers to bolster those qualities within themselves.

When Lenny taught karate to his students, the lesson went way beyond mere physical training. "I taught mental stability," said Lenny. Most informed people know that karate is not a sport, it is a discipline.

More specifically, it involves self-discipline, which learned in karate does not allow a negative thought to exist.

Lenny was asked if he had any advice for people who suffer from excessive worrying. Lenny said, "It is clear and simple. With practice, we can learn to control our thinking and attitude, and not allow the worrisome thoughts to exist." Lenny's key message to his students was to never give up hope. Psychiatric professionals testify that the key ingredient in suicide is that a person has a sense of hopelessness. "I had this already going through this," said Lenny, pointing to the two stubs of his amputated legs, but he never gave in to that temporary hopelessness.

Looking back to his recent medical crisis losing both his legs and hearing physicians say he should have died months earlier ,Lenny said, "I have had plenty of nights like that." Nights when someone without Lenny's strength, courage, and patience would have easily have allowed hopelessness to win.

When you are dealing with adversity, whether it be a karate fight with a difficult opponent or a pile of difficult paperwork toward the end of a long day at work, you need to muster your inner strength, stay with it, and do not give up because you are a lot tougher than you think, be positive.

Lenny testified that he once had a near-death experience. In the year 2010, Lenny had a severe septic shock condition that put him in a coma for seven days. The blood infection started in his right stump and spread everywhere. "I lost the use of my kidneys and my family held a constant vigil by my bedside and my wife never left my side." When he awoke he said he saw his parents and they told him to go back it was not his time.

Lenny was in a very dark area and there was a light in the far distance and his mom said, go to the light and he did. When he awoke he was crying because he really missed his mom, he missed her dearly. Lenny said, "I would have loved to be with my parents but I have my wife here and my children that is why I was sent back." It took Lenny a long time to get over this near-death experience.

Throughout his severe medical challenges right up to the end of his life, Lenny continued to fight with the ferocity of a black belt karate champion, he never stopped, and he left this world a champion. Lenny passed away the month of February in the year 2012, and he is greatly missed by those who deeply love him and those who had the honor of knowing him. Lenny will always provide inspiration.

**Author's note: I also did not let hopelessness win with all the experiences growing up in the failed foster system and no love from my mother. I never let what happened in my childhood interfere with my future to care for my loved ones, my family can attest to that. I have not let adversity win, I stood strong through it all, like I said earlier, what does not kill you makes you stronger and I am a witness to that.*

"New Found Freedom"

I recently took a trip upstate, as I do often, to visit my three daughters and a few grandchildren. I told them about the story I am writing, and I gave them an unrevised copy to read. My grand godson said I should elaborate more, of which I did. I stayed a week like I always do. The biggest thing about coming home after my trip was that I was thinking about my antique carriage, my dolls, antique crib, and more.

With the blink of an eye, I decided to sell them or donate them. This felt like a new-found freedom I have never felt before, letting go of these items I have kept all these years, because of the memories and feelings when I was four years old in that tiny house. Letting go of all those special items and writing my story is a great release from my past.

It was not easy going through all the traumatic experiences of the past. All I can say I wanted to be the best mom I could be, something I never had. Not having a mom and dad does affect you all through your life, but I do the best I can and always try and do more. It is not what you have been through in your life, but how you come out of it, and I came out of it pretty good, thanks to me.

"The Black Crow"

After I completed typing my story, I left the computer room to relax on the couch. A few seconds later ,I heard this really loud bang and glass shatter. I looked around the entire house and then I looked in the computer room and found that the window alongside the computer was shattered.

I called the police to have an officer sent over just in case it was some kind of vandalism in the neighborhood. Turns out the officer said it was a black crow that hit the window; it was laying in the area where the window shattered. I really feel that some supernatural force caused the crow to go into the window right where I was typing. Was this because I finally opened up after all these years and let it be known what my sister and I went through with my mother, grandmother, and the foster parents? Somehow, the crow let me know that the ones that did abuse us knew I was telling my story.

"The Symbol of the Black Crow"

Crows symbolize transformation and change. They are watchful creatures that have a sharp and powerful foresight. If you cross a crow and think of it as an adverse outcome, then this is just one of the many possible results. But much more than this, the crow refers more to spiritual and emotional change.

These intelligent birds give us valuable insights to situations around us and help us adapt as needed. So you see, the crow hit my window where I was typing, signifying emotional and spiritual change for me. I will adapt to the new-found freedom now that I have told my story, which also includes Lenny's story.

www.ingramcontent.com/pod-product-compliance
Lightning Source LLC
Chambersburg PA
CBHW052210150726
48002CB00003B/1161